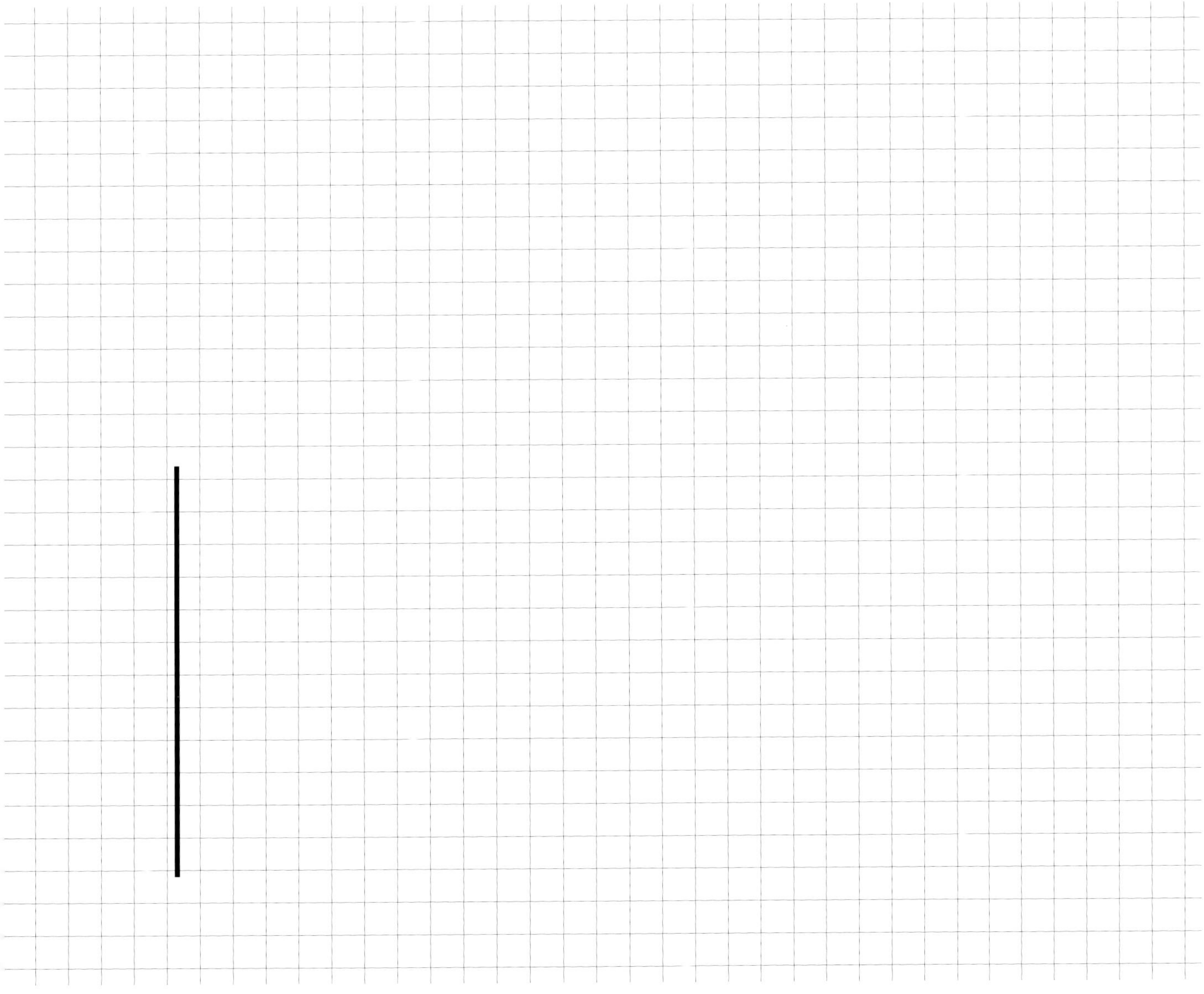

ƧA, THEN

PETER DOWNSBROUGH

AS,

ИƎHT

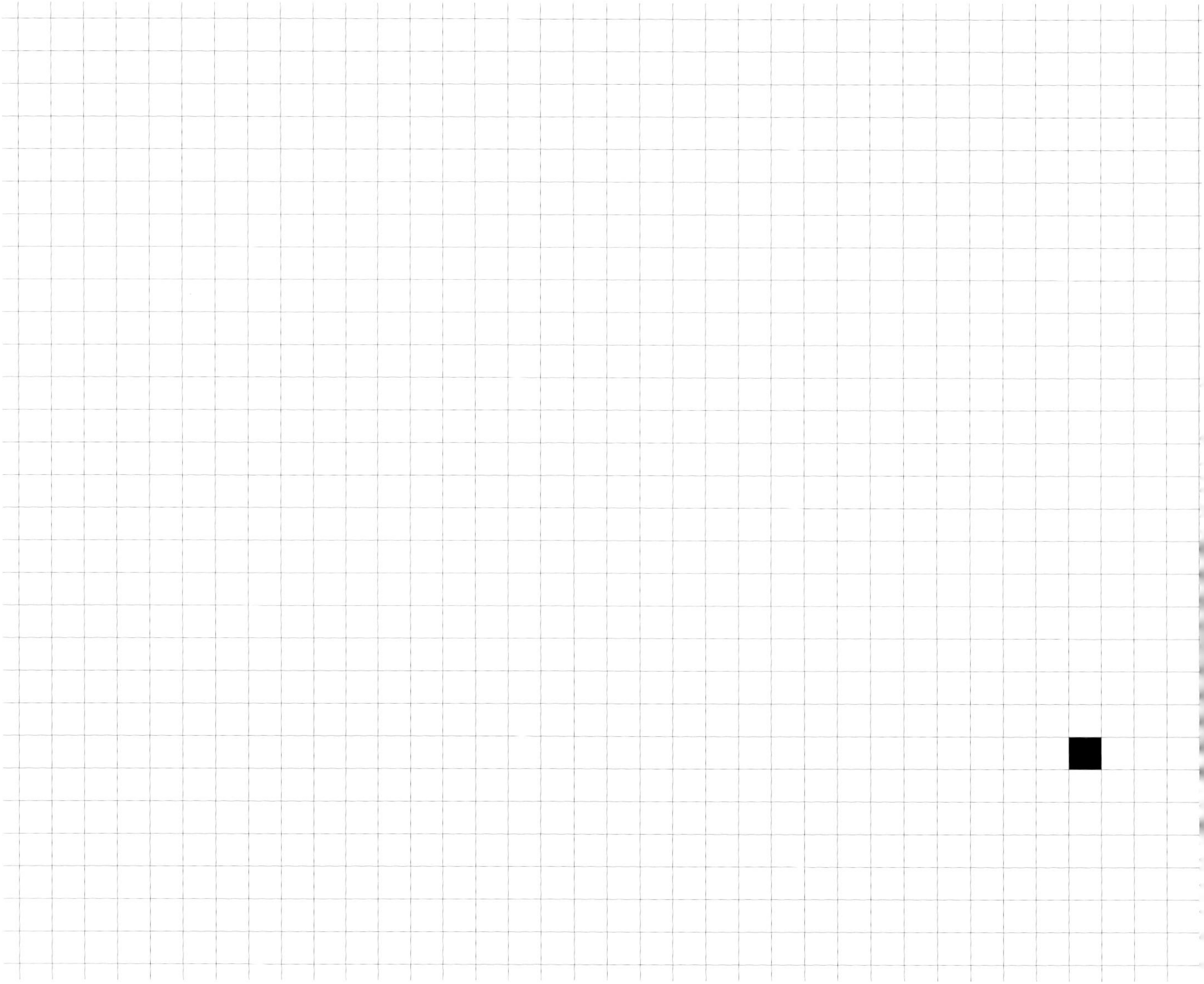

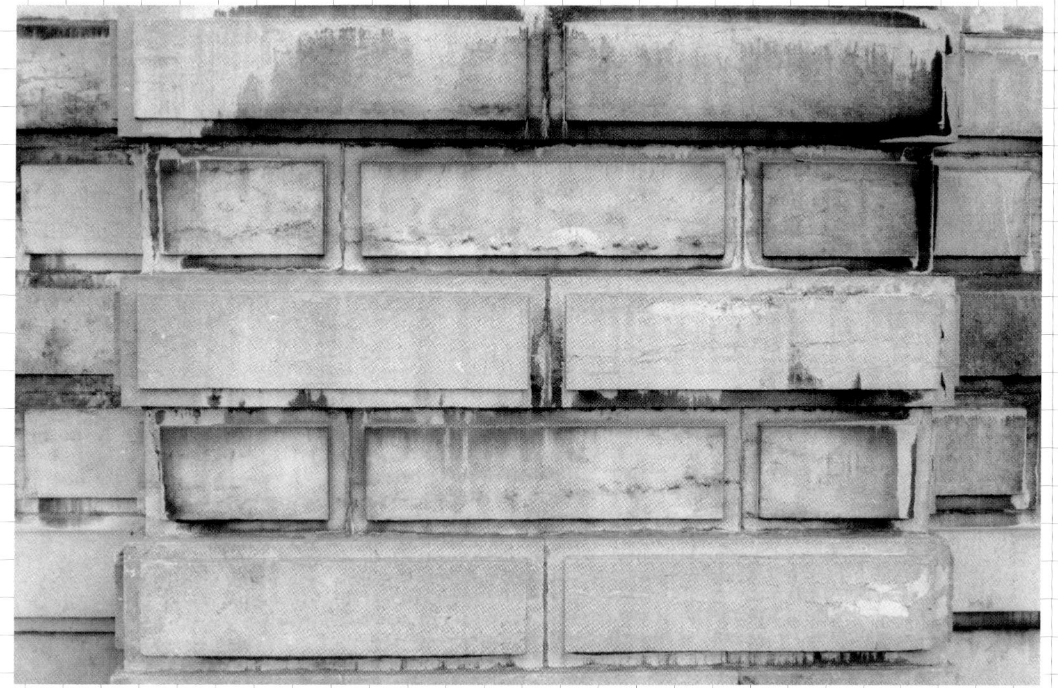

AND

THEN

SETTLE

THERE

AND

DISPLACE

THERE | HERE

AS

THE

LINK

OTHER

TRACE

THE

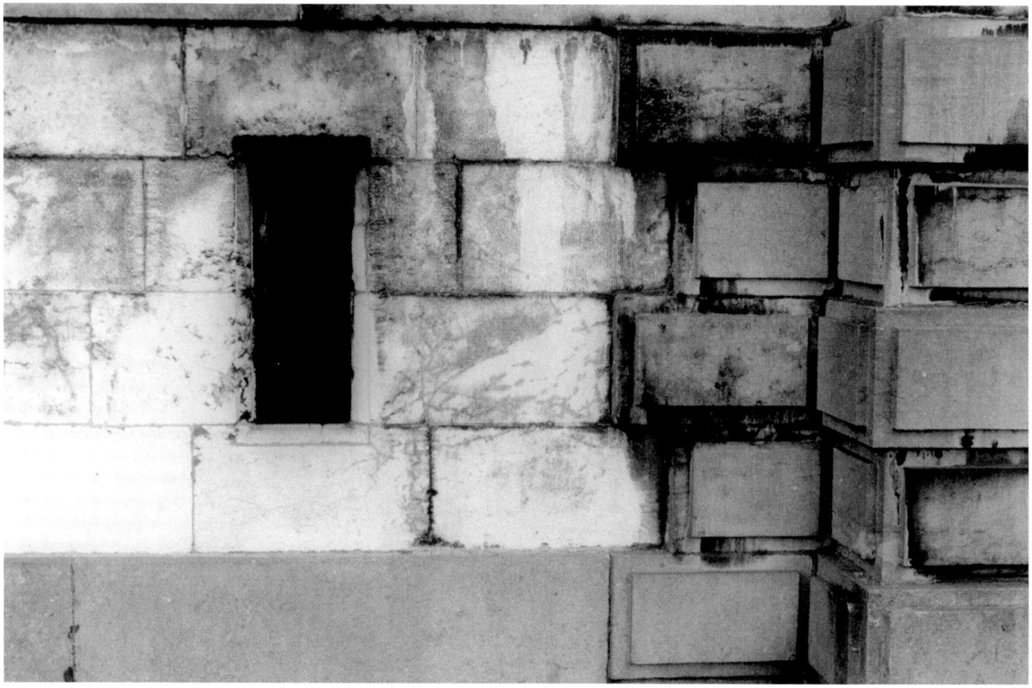

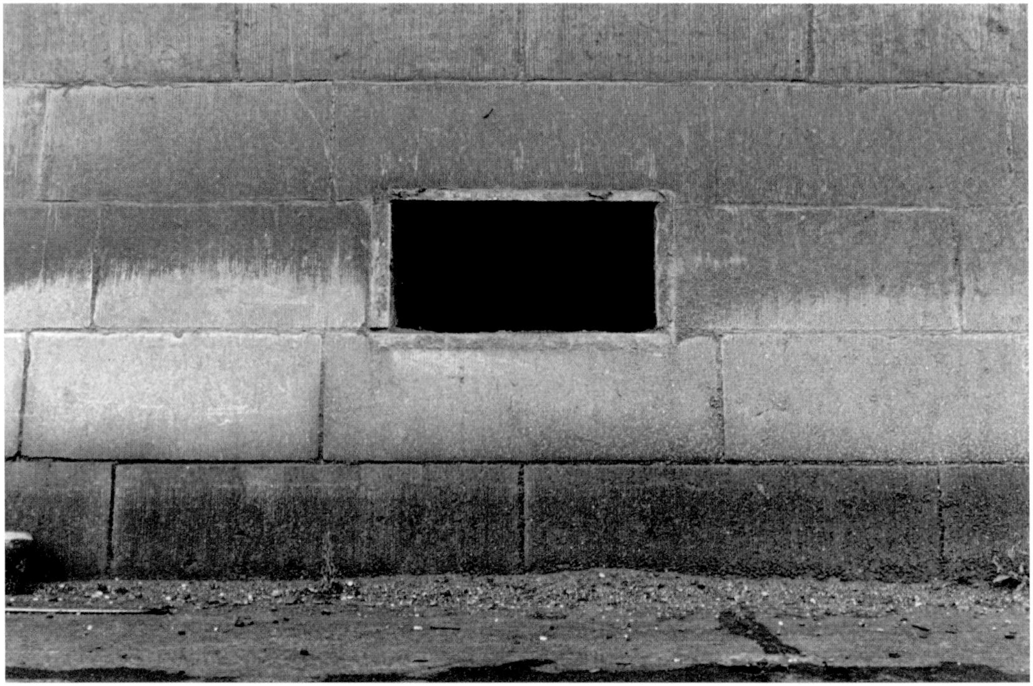

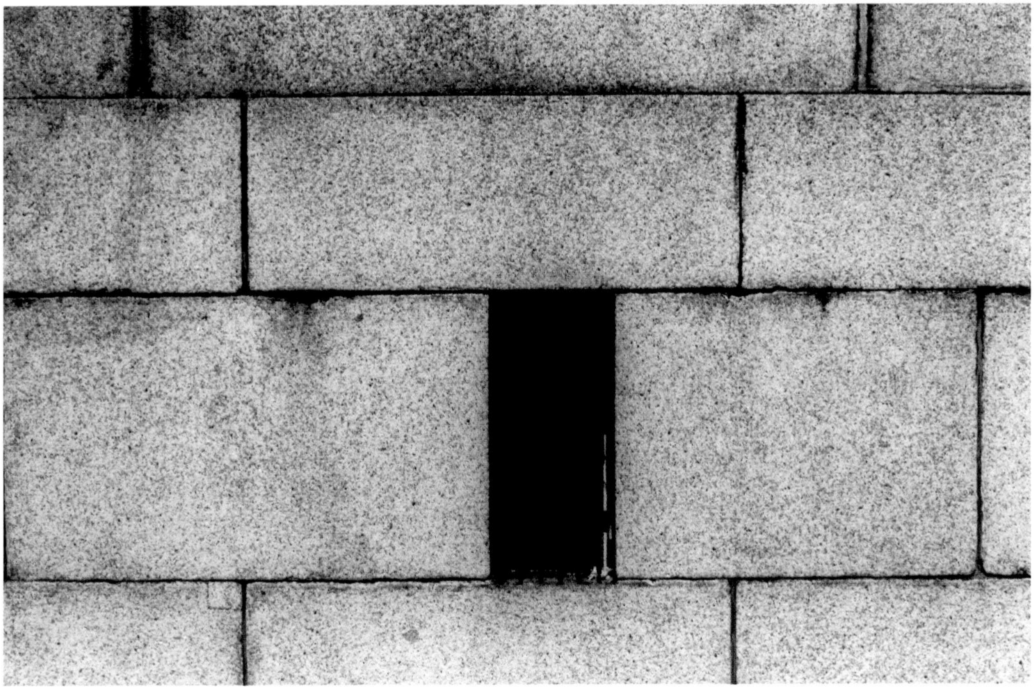

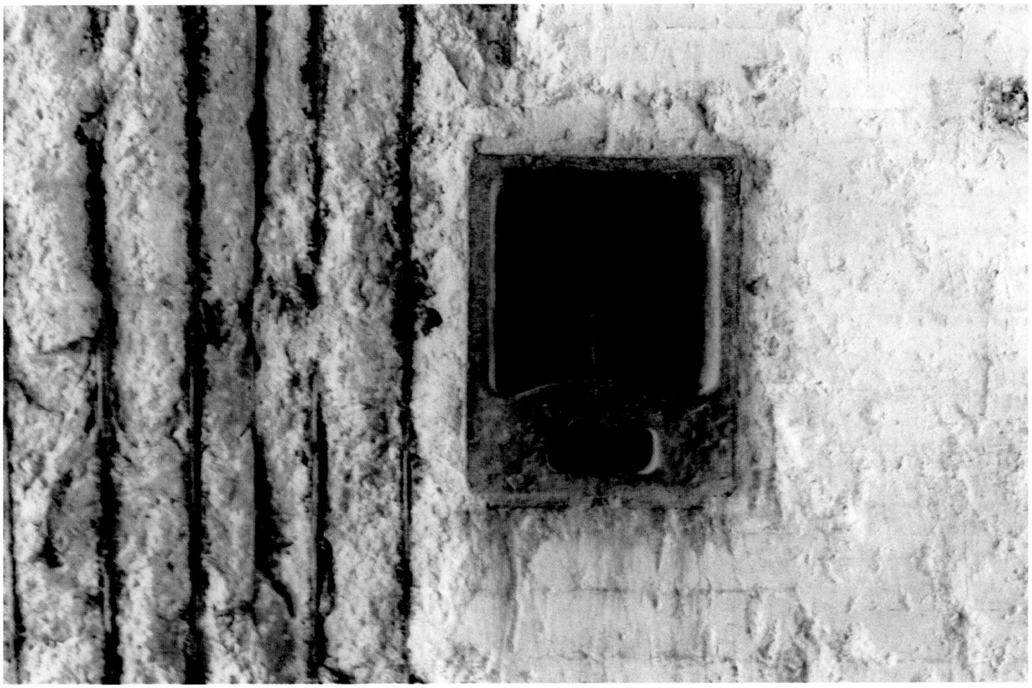

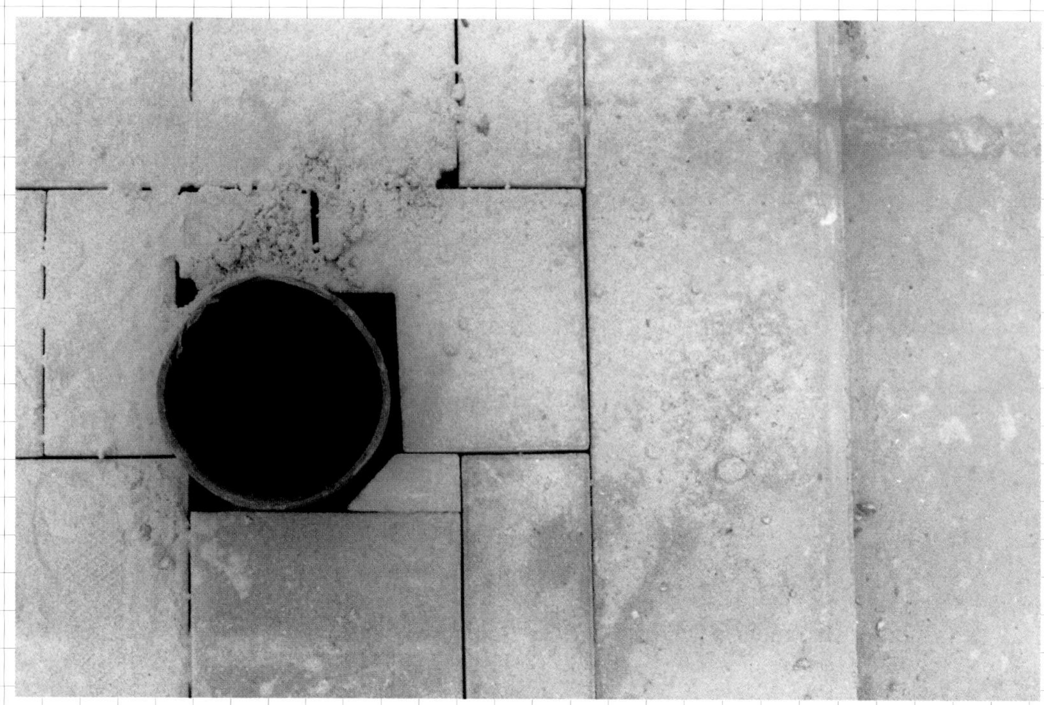

SHIFT

BETWEEN

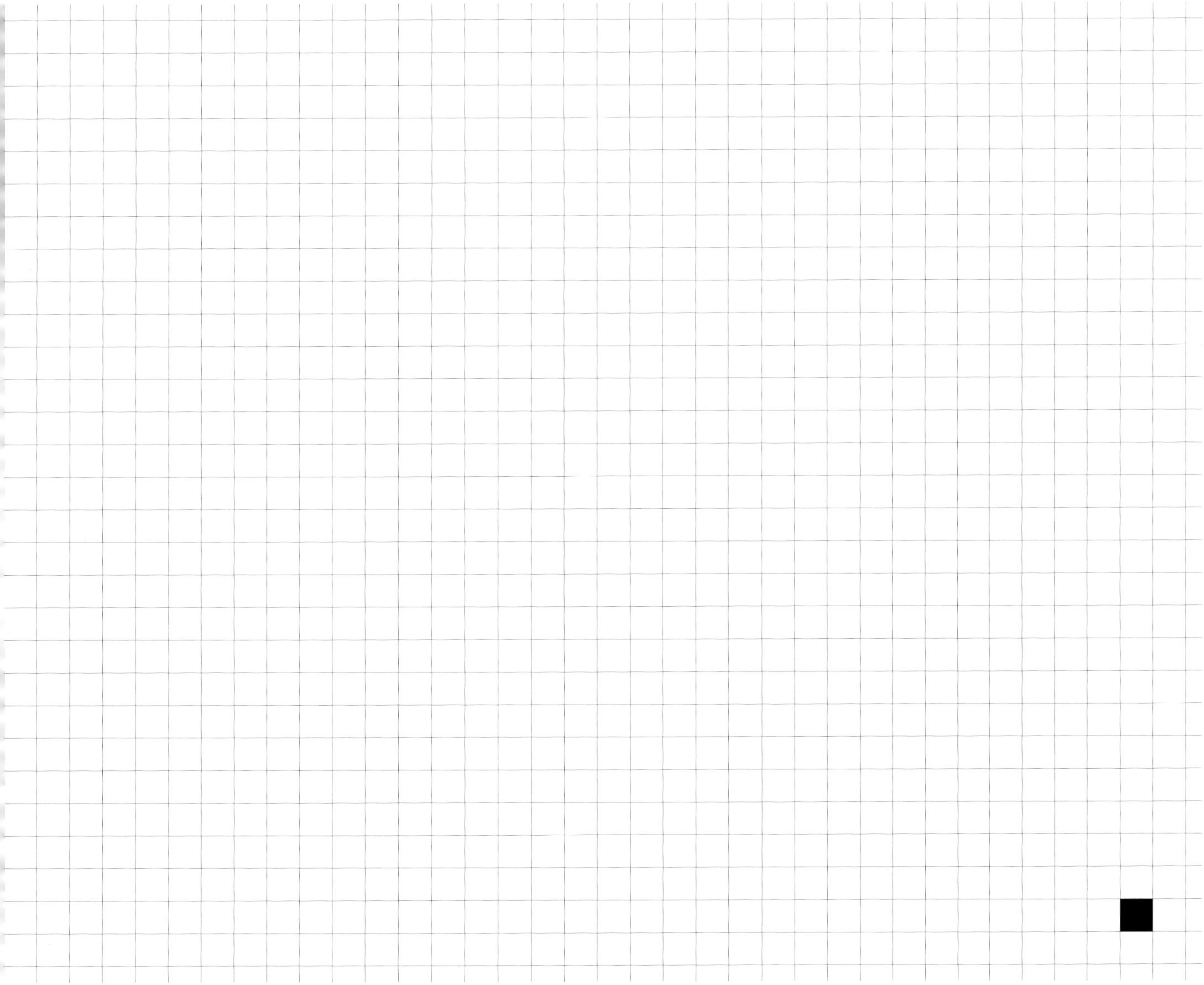

PLACE

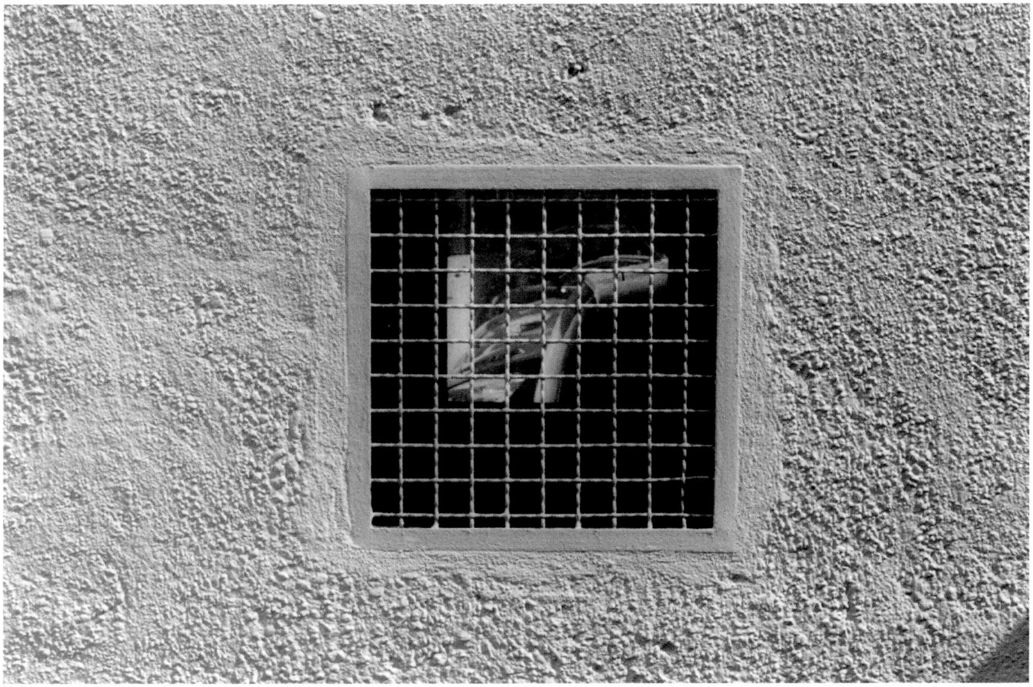

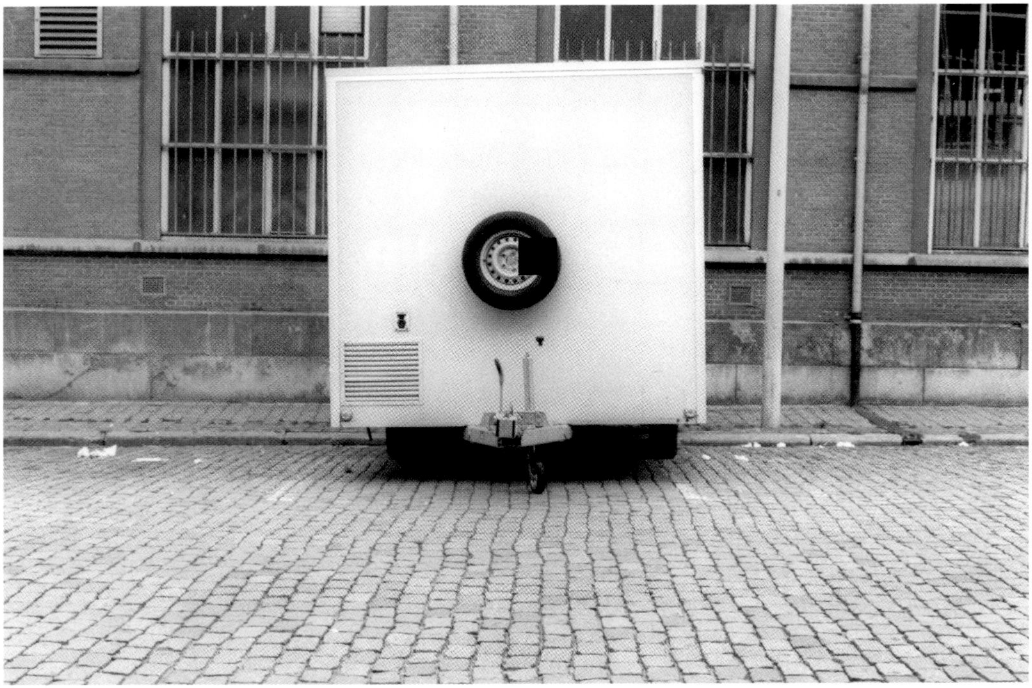

___ TIME, JUST FOLDED IN